CHINESE
ETIQUETTE

CHINESE ETIQUETTE

ETIQUETTE

A Matter of Course

Raelene Tan

Currency values in this book are in Singapore dollars

Copyright © Raelene Tan 1992
Fourth Impression October 1998
Illustrations by Felicia Chan

LANDMARK BOOKS PTE LTD
5001, Beach Road, #02-73/74, Singapore 0719

ISBN 981-3002-57-3

Films processed by Superskill Graphics Pte Ltd
Printed by Loi Printing Pte Ltd

TABLE OF CONTENTS

ACKNOWLEDGEMENTS

*My patient husband and children deserve
kudos for putting up with my long and erratic
hours of research.*

*Ms Violet Oon is to be commended for her
faith in me and for encouraging me to write.
Others who deserve special thanks for their
invaluable assistance are Mr Tan Eng Ho,
Ms Mary Tan Mui Lee, Mr S.R. Tan, Dr George
Tay and all those persons whose table manners
I observed without their realising.*

AUTHOR'S PREFACE

When I was approached to write a series of books on table etiquette, I had no idea that it would be such an immense task — enjoyable but daunting.

Table etiquette alone does not carry one far enough, I feel, unless there is also a knowledge of what goes into the occasion, whether it be a visit to a friend's home, a wedding reception or a business gathering. That is why special occasions have been touched upon in this book.

Chinese Etiquette – A Matter of Course is not meant to be a guide to customs and traditions, but rather a guide to good food etiquette as pertaining to the various types of Chinese cuisine.

The removing of shoes before entering homes, various superstitions and the importance of colours and numbers are all important common factors among the various Chinese dialect groups. Since they are not the usual practices for many non-Asians, they are mentioned where relevant.

Faux pas also cover the whole spectrum, from Westerners unwittingly ordering and eating individual dishes of Asian food, as they would Western dishes, to mishandling chopsticks and wearing black or sombre clothing to auspicious functions.

If one does find oneself caught in an awkward situation, the important thing to remember is that it can be salvaged. Either make a little joke about it, or simply eat humble pie and apologise sincerely.

Here are some bits to chew on.

It is better to plead ignorance than to offend. No one will get upset when you humbly mention beforehand that you do not know something.

Ask and you will be told. Others are usually willing to help and show what they know.

If you cannot ask, then watch. Copy the actions of someone who knows what to do.

Having manners simply means being thoughtful towards others, and showing respect and tolerance. If we are considerate in our attitude, we can never offend or hurt others.

The aim of this book, therefore, is to make cross-cultural interaction, especially at social occasions, even more pleasureable. It is also for people in business who entertain clients from different cultural backgrounds.

Without help and encouragement from my friends, this book could not have been completed. I asked so many questions, they patiently replied, cooked and demonstrated and asked me questions in return. I wrangled invitations to homes, restaurants, wedding receptions, babies' one-month celebrations, business gatherings, to prod, pry and question. My knowledge increased, as well as my waistline!

It must be said here that this is not a book of strict rules. It is simply my hope that *Chinese Etiquette – A Matter of Course* helps to answer questions on Chinese table and social etiquette.

Raelene Tan
1992

CHINESE ETIQUETTE

The Chinese, wherever they have settled, have contributed much in the way of fine cuisine and the rich and varied art forms stemming from their long history.

Within the Chinese community as a whole, there are smaller communities comprising people of various dialect groups (such as Hokkien, Cantonese, Teochew, Hakka, Hainanese), harking back to their individual origins in China. A different tongue is spoken by each group, but the written language is common to all.

Traditionally, the Chinese are, in the main, believers of Buddhism and Taoism, with some being Confucian in thought.

Buddhism was founded in the sixth century B.C. in India. Buddhists believe in reincarnation and follow the teachings of the Buddha. They aspire to reach Nirvana (enlightenment) through self-denial and righteous living. Meditation is often practised.

Taoism (the way) was founded about the sixth century B.C. by Lao-tzu and teaches that heaven and earth were made to move in unison, or harmony (a balance of *yin* and *yang*), and that the natural, simple life and selflessness are the ways to find fulfilment.

CONFUCIUS

China's most famous teacher and philosopher, Confucius, left a legacy of ethical values (including the virtues of filial piety, magnanimity and righteousness) to shape the way of life, and his thoughts have influenced Chinese and other Asian societies for over 2,000 years.

Traditional Chinese customs and practices are complex because of the different dialect groups and religious beliefs, therefore the details of etiquette vary from group to group. However, the etiquette mentioned in this book should be adequate for most Chinese social functions, bearing in mind slight variations among different families.

SOCIETY

The Chinese believe that the family is the cornerstone of society. Filial piety and respect for the elders are highly valued and extended families are common. They are hard-working and have a long history of culture and traditions of which they are justly proud. The Chinese are astute businessmen and live relatively simple lives.

CALENDAR

The Chinese calendar is based on the moon, with the New Year celebrated on the first day of the first moon, in January or February.

GREETINGS

On meeting Chinese people these days, a hand-shake is acceptable for greeting and parting for both males and females. However, note that Buddhist monks do not shake hands with, or touch, women, and Buddhist nuns do not shake hands.

A traditional Chinese greeting is to clasp both hands together, left hand over the right fist, and make a few gentle up and down movements by flexing the wrists downwards with the clasped hands at chest level, at the same time giving a nod of the head. A simple nod is also an acceptable greeting.

"Have you eaten yet?", a common opening remark, is not really a question, and the reply may be a simple, "Yes, thank you", even if you haven't!

NAMES

Chinese names are apt to cause confusion among foreigners, but they are really quite simple to understand.

The surname is placed first, then the generation name and lastly the given name, as in Tan Li Nian, who is the son of Tan Soo Ken. Tan is the surname, Li is the generation name, meaning that all his brothers and male cousins may have 'Li' after the surname. This makes it easy to identify a distinct family lineage. Lastly, Nian is his own given name. However, note that sometimes the last two names — generation and given — are transposed. Tan Li Nian would be addressed as Mr. Tan, although his friends may call him Li Nian or just Nian. As a new acquaintance, be careful not to use just the given name unless asked to.

FEMALE NAME

The same style of name applies to Chinese females, although males and females of the same generation usually have different root names. You may address, say, Chen Lu Lene as Miss Chen, or more familiarly as Lu Lene or just Lene. A married Chinese lady

MARRIED NAME

does not necessarily take her husband's name upon marriage, but sometimes retains her own surname and adds the title 'Madam'. So from being the single Miss Chen Lu Lene she becomes the married Madam Chen Lu Lene, even though she married Mr Tan Li Nian. However, it is common to address married women with their husband's surname, as in Mrs Tan.

CHILDREN'S NAMES

Children take their father's surname.

INTRODUCTIONS

ORDER OF INTRODUCTIONS

When performing introductions in the Chinese manner, the older or most respected person's name is mentioned first and a gentleman's name before a lady's.

Chinese family members should be greeted according to age, beginning with the oldest.

FORM OF ADDRESS FOR OLDER PERSONS

Asians in general usually address any older persons as 'Aunty' or 'Uncle'. Do not be surprised at this if you are not a relative.

It is simply a form of respect. If you, in turn, address elders in a likewise manner you will be extending politeness.

VISITING A CHINESE HOME

Most Chinese are informal and enjoy inviting friends to eat with them whether at home, in a restaurant, or hawker centre. Their inherent love of food, and the wide variety of Chinese cuisine available, makes an invitation to eat, whether at home or out, something to be looked forward to.

When you are invited to a Chinese home, first ascertain the time you are expected and then endeavour to be punctual, though guests should never arrive earlier than the stipulated time. In fact, Chinese guests almost always arrive late.

Upon arrival, it is customary to remove your shoes and leave them at the door. If the host indicates that shoes can be worn indoors, they are not worn in a bedroom, in order to keep the floor clean.

An altar can sometimes be seen in a Chinese home. Some altars are devoted to family ancestors and some are for praying to deities. The latter are red and have images of gods or a goddess although both have a joss-stick holder placed in a prominent position. Other items which may be seen on altars are small tea cups and a teapot, rice bowls filled with uncooked rice grains, and oranges, sugar cane, flowers and lampstands. A polite guest will not touch the items on the altar. If curious, a few simple questions addressed to the host will no doubt bring satisfaction.

Some Chinese believe that by placing a mirror above the entrance door, or outdoors above a window, evil spirits will be warded off, frightened by the light of their own reflections, and that the mirror will counteract unfavourable outside influences.

Do not sit until your Chinese host invites you to do so.

As a guest, you should sit to the left of your host as a mark of respect to him, although you should be sensitive to the host's wishes, especially when there are other guests present.

Try to keep your legs still whilst sitting. Leg-shaking is believed to shake off good luck.

It is wise to practise decorum, as Chinese appreciate fine ways.

When you call on a Chinese family, whether unexpectedly or not, you will almost certainly be served a drink, often Chinese tea. Do drink at least a little, as it is most impolite not to do so.

In the Chinese way, when giving and receiving an item, two hands should always be used — for instance when giving or accepting a drink, a plate of food or even a newspaper.

When an older person enters the room, it

is usual to rise. Always remember to greet older people ('Aunty' or 'Uncle'), even without an introduction.

To beckon in the presence of Chinese, you should wave your right hand, fingers outstretched downwards, and the palm facing inwards towards your body.

If you wish to point in the presence of Chinese, extend your right arm and hand in front of your body, palm facing towards the left, and fingers together.

When passing in front of a Chinese person, or persons, it is polite to bow slightly whilst walking and say, "Excuse me".

Refrain from body-touching as it is not considered proper. Head-touching, especially of children, is also not good form.

When taking leave of a Chinese family, it is polite to say goodbye to all persons present in the house (except at funeral wakes).

DRESS

The *cheongsam* (literally, in Cantonese, 'long-dress') is the high Mandarin-collar dress, with side slits, that Chinese women look so good in. The *samfu* (literally, in Cantonese, 'dress-pants') is the pantsuit that some Chinese ladies favour.

Nowadays, Western-style clothes are commonly worn by Chinese females.

Chinese males these days mostly wear trousers and shirts.

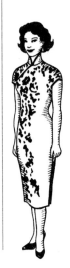

Do, of course, remember to dress modestly when with Chinese people and choose clothes that are not all-white or all-black as they are traditionally for mourning.

I well remember a European friend wearing her best black dress, with pearls, to a Chinese wedding dinner and almost being ostracized by all present! Her husband, Chinese and a doctor, had spent so long overseas studying that, on that particular occasion, he had simply overlooked his wife's dress, and almost caused a family rift!

All-dark-blue and all-green are also associated by the Chinese with death, so do take care with your dressing, both males and females, if you do not wish to offend.

Red is the colour signifying good luck within the Chinese community, with pink, orange and yellow also favoured, and wearing such colours to formal functions is most appropriate.

For a formal Chinese function, such as a wedding or business dinner, if the style of dress preferred is not mentioned on the invitation card, you should check with your host when you are uncertain. Usually a long-sleeved shirt with tie, or a safari suit, is acceptable for gentlemen, with ladies dressed in conformity. A national costume is always appropriate.

If in doubt, at any time, by all means telephone the restaurant or your Chinese host and enquire.

CONVERSATION

Chinese practise modesty of speech when referring to themselves and their families, in an almost deprecating manner.

DEPRECATING SPEECH

Chinese hosts are well-known for 'running down' the food served to their guests, even in a grand restaurant, simply because they feel their guests are always worthy of more and better!

Such questions, even to mere acquaintances, as, "How much did it cost?", "What is your salary?" and, "How old are you?" are not intended to be prying, but are commonly asked by Asians of different ethnic groups, including Chinese. Non-Asians find such questions downright rude and this can lead to misunderstandings. Both sides should try and compromise by being aware of these differences.

'PRYING' QUESTIONS

Unless your Chinese host raises the subjects, it is best to steer clear of sex, politics and religion. As many Chinese are superstitious, endeavour to avoid the subject of death.

TABOO SUBJECTS

Food is a favourite topic, and places to eat and shop are dear to the hearts of most Chinese. Complimenting the host's country is a wise move. Sports and movies also make for easy conversation.

SAFE SUBJECTS

INVITATIONS

Of course all invitations, written and personal, must be acknowledged as soon as possible, whether accepting or declining.

Red and pink are auspicious colours for invitation cards, though nowadays pastel colours are also quite common. As a general guide, if you receive a bright red invitation card, then you can expect a more traditional function.

If you are sending an invitation card to a member of the Chinese community, try not to choose a plain white or plain blue card (or white and blue) as these colours are used for funerals. If your cards are white, you might like to choose gold or red printing, rather than black.

Foreign businessmen, in particular, should be aware of the importance of colours to the Chinese in this respect.

Where RSVP and a telephone number are given together on the invitation card, then a telephoned reply is in order, whether accepting or declining. Often response cards are enclosed with invitations.

THANK YOU

A verbal thank you when leaving a function is normally sufficient. A telephone call to your Chinese host or hostess, within a day or two of the function, is a nice thought by a guest, as is a thank-you note, although they are not necessities. Flowers are not normally sent.

GIFTS AND OCCASIONS

GENERAL CONSIDERATIONS

Gifts are always a nice thought, but care should be taken not to upset by a poor choice. They must be presented and received, in the Chinese way, by using two hands.

PRESENTING A GIFT

Should you receive a present from your Chinese friend, express thanks but do not open it in front of the giver.

OPENING A GIFT

Red and gold are the colours to choose when selecting wrapping-paper and bows for gifts for Chinese friends, as both colours signify good luck.

COLOURS FOR GIFT WRAPPING

Gifts should be prepared in even numbers as odd numbers are frowned upon. Generally, circular items such as oranges, crockery, drinking glasses, tinned biscuits and the like are auspicious, since roundness signifies completeness.Food is an acceptable gift at most occasions.

NUMBER AND SHAPE OF GIFTS

A gift of money is acceptable, whatever the function, and it is always presented in an envelope with the name of the giver endorsed on the back of the envelope. For an

A GIFT OF MONEY

AUSPICIOUS
OCCASIONS

FUNERAL

EVEN OR ODD
AMOUNT

AMOUNT OF
CASH FOR A GIFT

SUPERSTITIONS

auspicious occasion, a red envelope *(hong bao)*, available at most departmental stores, is always used. When presenting money at a Chinese funeral, a plain white envelope must be used. What is important, is to ensure that the amount presented is in an even number for an auspicious occasion, and in an uneven number for a funeral.

A gift of money is used by the recipient to help offset the cost of the particular function. There is no 'correct amount', though the amount is usually comparable to the cost of the individual meal provided.

Superstitions play a role in everyday life for many Chinese folk, so care should be taken by non-Chinese not to unwittingly upset a friend or colleague.

The various dialect groups have their own superstitions about numbers. The Cantonese and Hokkien believe that the number four has bad connotations due to it sounding like the word 'dead' in those dialects. Six is a number surrounded by luck and eight and eighty-eight represent 'prosperity' and 'double prosperity' respectively for many Chinese people, again because of phonic associations.

I remember vividly a mistake at a family birthday party for my Hokkien mother-in-law. A Western guest, married to a Chinese businessman who was a nephew of the guest-of-honour, purchased a porcelain vase as a gift, hand-painted with flowers and a long-legged bird. The unfortunate woman did not show the item to her husband, simply mentioning to him that she had purchased a vase, and dutifully wrapped it in red paper.

At the party, some guests were discussing the gifts they had presented to the grand old lady (who, incidentally, was not enjoying good health at the time) and everybody froze when the painted vase was mentioned.

The long-legged bird painted on the vase looked like a heron, or maybe a stork, and the Hokkiens believe that the heron is a symbol of a woman's death!

Fortunately gifts are not opened in public by the Chinese — the offending item was quickly retrieved and the shocked husband of the poor woman who bought the vase was despatched post-haste to buy a suitable replacement.

All was well that ended well. If, by coincidence, anything untoward had happened to the would-be recipient, the unsuspecting guest might have been blamed!

Other items to avoid giving to Chinese friends are knives and scissors (they may sever a friendship), clocks (the Cantonese word for clock is phonetically the same as 'funeral'), handkerchiefs (often given to persons attending a funeral and suggesting tears) and items in sombre colours. It is also best not to give any white flowers as a gift.

TABOO GIFTS

SPECIFIC OCCASIONS AND GIFTS

For a first-time visit to a Chinese home, it is not necessary to take a gift and your host or hostess will not expect anything, as they look upon you as an honoured guest. However, if you feel that you cannot go empty-handed, then a gift of sweets expressly for the children could be taken.

HOME-COOKED MEAL

For a specific occasion, such as when invited by Chinese friends for a home-cooked meal, sweets, fruit (especially oranges and apples), biscuits and brandy are well thought of — remember to give in pairs or even numbers (that is, two items though not necessarily the same). The giving of flowers is not usual.

Sometimes, upon the guest leaving, the Chinese host will return in kind part of the gift to reciprocate good luck.

NEW-BORN BABY

The birth of a baby is extremely important as it continues the family line. If you are giving a gift on the occasion of a new-born baby, it is customary to present a gift to the new mother or the baby, or both. Appropriate items for the mother would be nourishing food such as chicken essence, tonic wine, fruit, biscuits or noodles. For the baby, gold jewellery, clothing, toiletries or toys would be suitable.

As with some other communities, home visits are not encouraged during the first month after birth as mother and baby require rest. If you wish, you may visit at the hospital, or wait until after the one-month confinement period and then telephone in advance to ask if it is convenient for you to visit the home.

The 'full-moon' celebration, when baby is one month old, is a very important occasion. Red eggs (hard-boiled hens' eggs with the shells dyed red) and round cakes are some of the items distributed to relatives and friends who presented gifts during the confinement period, on this auspicious occasion. Red eggs represent new life and good luck. The roundness of the cakes represents family unity.

An appropriate gift at an engagement party would be a household article or an item for the bride-to-be's *trousseau*. An engagement ring, often a diamond ring, is given to the girl by her betrothed, to be worn on the ring finger of her left hand. The wearing of a ring by her *fiance* is optional. It is appropriate for guests to admire the ring or rings. The newly engaged couple often distribute cakes and sweets (featuring the colour red for good luck) to friends and relatives to announce their happy news.

For a marriage ceremony, an appropriate wedding gift would be gold jewellery or household items in cheery colours, although it is quite usual to give money in a red envelope *(hongbao)* — remember to give in pairs or in even numbers and to use two hands for the giving. The gift may be presented to the bride or groom or to an usher at the wedding dinner.

TEA CEREMONY

The Chinese wedding usually involves a traditional tea ceremony which is a family affair of great importance. The giving and receiving of cups of Chinese tea, by the bridal couple to their older relatives, signifies respect for the older family members by the newly-weds, and their acceptance into the family by the relatives. *Hongbao* and/or jewellery are presented to the bridal couple by the relatives, after the tea has been drunk, during this ceremony. Tea is served according to seniority, beginning with the eldest member of the family.

Guests may observe that, following Western practice, the wedding ring is worn by the bride on the ring finger of her left hand. It is optional for the bridegroom to wear a wedding ring, and if he does, it is also worn on the ring finger of his left hand.

WEDDING DINNER

It is usual for friends to be invited to the wedding dinner, in a restaurant, which is the culmination of a busy day for the bride and groom and their close relatives.

PUNCTUALITY

Chinese wedding dinners are notorious for commencing later than the stipulated time. I'm a stickler for punctuality and am often the only guest in sight (with my long-suffering husband) for forty-five minutes or more!

SEATING

If there is no formal seating arrangement, guests should rely on an usher, or, if there is no usher, simply look for a familiar face at a table and ask to join that table.

When guests meet the bride and groom at the reception, guests should offer congratulations and avoid any talk of disaster or sickness.

At the wedding dinner, during the feast, the bridal couple and their retinue will go from table to table (there are usually ten persons seated at each round table and there may be hundreds of guests) and guests will rise and wish them well by toasting with their drinks to the long drawn-out shouts of "*Yam Seng*" (Cantonese, drink for success). The glass is held in both hands and the glass should be held up high. The groom will fill guests' glasses, where necessary.

TOASTING

The newly married couple will be seated with their parents at the main table, which is normally resplendent with a red table-cloth. A number of courses will be served, usually eight or ten.

Rice is served at weddings to represent plenty. A whole fish is an auspicious dish served to represent prosperity and harmony. Therefore for such an occasion, the head and tail are left intact so as not to break up good fortune.

AUSPICIOUS FARE

Chinese tea is always available, as tea trees are capable of living for a century or more, firmly rooted in one place, thereby symbolising longevity and marital fidelity.

The evening closes as soon as the last

course is eaten, there is no lingering. The bridal party will shake hands with guests, at the exit.

BIRTHDAY

For a birthday party, the same etiquette applies pertaining to gifts, dress and eating as for other happy occasions within the Chinese community. Noodles are traditionally served, representing longevity. Care must be taken not to cut the noodles when serving, in deference to the symbolic value. Buns, made of dough with a sweet bean-paste filling, in the shape of peaches, are often seen in a pyramid-shaped arrangement, especially at parties for older Chinese persons. The peach is a symbol of long life, and the buns are equivalent to the Western birthday cake.

HOUSEWARMING

A housewarming dinner is often given when a Chinese family moves to their new home. Relatives and friends are invited and dinner is often buffet style, with dishes such as noodles and meat or fish balls (for longevity and harmony) served. A suitable gift would be a household item, though not knives, scissors or clocks.

FUNERAL

If confronted with the necessity to attend the funeral of a Chinese person, a floral wreath may be sent to the home or funeral parlour. If you prefer, money in uneven numbers ($11, $21, $35 and the like) may be given to the family, presented in a white envelope, or a donation may be made, at the wake, to a charitable organisation if one is

FLORAL/ MONETARY CONTRIBUTION

specified by the family.

White, black or sombre colours should be worn when visiting the home or funeral parlour to pay respects. Jewellery and bright make-up are not appropriate. Often, family members of the deceased will wear special mourning garments. A patch of dark cloth pinned on a sleeve indicates that the person is in mourning.

APPROPRIATE ATTIRE

After approaching the family of the deceased, it is customary to view the body — stand at the foot of the coffin and make a mark of respect, such as three bows.

You do not need to use joss-sticks if you do not wish to; simply shake your head briefly when offered the sticks. If you do use joss-sticks and they flare up, the flame should be put out by gently fanning with the hand, not blown out. A bow to the mourning family members, who keep a vigil at the side of the coffin, is then made.

JOSS -STICKS

Cremation, or burial, can be three, five or seven days after death, in order to allow time for friends and relatives to come together to offer condolences and pay their respects. Members of the family keep a constant vigil during this time. The preferred time for visitors is from 7 p.m. and into the late evening, in order to keep the family company.

FUNERAL WAKE

Lengthy, noisy, traditional ceremonies mark death, and family members of the deceased are sometimes expected to show their bereavement by crying and wailing.

After viewing the deceased, it is normal for visitors to stay and partake of food and drink. Sweets will be available on the tables at the wake and it is customary for a visitor to eat a sweet to counteract bitterness. If coins in red packets are given to visitors, it is for the purpose of buying sweets on the way home, to counteract evil. When at the home or funeral parlour, a family member will give visitors a length of red thread each. This can be wound around the visitor's button or handbag. Some threads are not colour-fast, so check to avoid staining your clothes. The red thread is to protect the visitor from ill-luck and traditionally the thread should be disposed of before the person enters his own home.

On the day of the funeral itself, visitors will sometimes be given a handkerchief each, signifying sadness. It is important not to be late for a funeral procession.

TAKING LEAVE

It is best not to say goodbye to the bereaved family, at the wake or the funeral, but rather to leave quietly.

TEMPLE

Anyone who enters a Chinese temple for any reason must behave in a reverent manner. Modest dressing is essential. Watch how worshippers behave, as different temples practise different customs. Do obtain permission before taking photographs. It is customary to enter a Chinese temple through the right door and to leave via the left door.

Dining Etiquette

PRE-MEAL

Relaxed conversation, in the living room, usually precedes a home-cooked meal, accompanied by Chinese tea and perhaps a snack such as watermelon seeds or nuts.

DRINKS AND SNACKS

SEATING AT THE TABLE

When you are eating in a Chinese restaurant, or at a private home, the host (or hostess), traditionally, will sit with his back to the entrance and the guest-of-honour will either be seated opposite the host (facing the entrance) or at the left side of the host.

SEATING

As a guest you should wait to be invited to sit. Men are often seated before women. When you eat with a family, the head of the family and his wife will normally sit together. Nowadays, seating arrangements are relatively informal.

Tables are usually circular, ideal for all persons to converse freely and to feel equal.

TABLE SETTINGS

In a Chinese home, serving platters of food

STYLE OF SERVICE

are placed in the centre of the table, with serving spoons.

There is often a turn-table in the centre of a round table, making for easy service of food.

WITH CHOPSTICKS Individual table settings vary from household to household, but, generally, there will be a rice bowl, with a pair of chopsticks and a chopsticks-rest to the right, a small flat plate (for placing food on), a soup bowl with a porcelain spoon, and a small dish for soya sauce and/or cut chillies placed to the right near the chopsticks.

WITH CUTLERY Alternatively, the setting may be a dinner plate with a fork to the left and a spoon to the right, and a soup bowl. With this setting, the spoon is used as the main eating utensil, including the eating of rice. Knives are not used, as Chinese food is served in bite-size portions.

FOR DRINKS A Chinese teacup or a glass will be placed to the top right of each setting.

Similar settings can be seen in Chinese restaurants.

BREAKFAST, LUNCH AND DINNER

A popular Chinese breakfast dish is a bowl of rice porridge *(congee)* accompanied by savoury foods such as minced pork, liver, chicken or fish, salted vegetable and eggs. This is also a popular lunch meal. Other breakfast favourites are fresh bread with jam and *yiu tiao* (long, curly, deep-fried dough sticks). The *yiu tiao*, also known as *yu char kway,* is finger food and it is often dunked in coffee.

Chinese tea, coffee and soya bean milk are the usual breakfast beverages.

A Chinese-style lunch often consists of a meat or fish dish with stir-fried vegetables and soup, or fried rice or fried noodles.

Fresh fruit is often served as a dessert.

Water, or Chinese tea, is the usual drink with lunch.

A *dian xin* or *tim sum* (tid-bit) lunch is ideal if you want to try a variety of tastes. The delicate food, mostly Cantonese style and steamed or deep-fried, is presented in small portions on small containers, often served from bamboo steamers, or sometimes in the steamer itself. Trolleys of cooked delicacies are sometimes pushed around the restaurant by serving staff. You simply ask for, or point to, whatever takes your fancy — dumplings, meat balls, buns, spring rolls, prawns, spare ribs, custard tarts, coconut pudding and many more varieties.

The food is shared amongst the party.

You help yourself to individual food items from the containers which are placed in the centre of the table. Using chopsticks, food should be taken from the serving container and brought to your plate first before being eaten.

Tim sum etiquette decrees that you only have one item of food on your plate at a time.

It's a great way to sample small portions of Chinese food from a large variety, at reasonable prices.

Using scissors, waitresses will cut food items if you so request, making it even easier to share the *tim sum* goodies.

When eating *bao* (a steamed white bun with a meat filling), fingers are in order both to peel off the paper on the base and to either break the *bao* in halves to eat, or to eat whole mouthful by mouthful.

Some food items are tricky to eat with chopsticks for the novice, including fish balls — so feel free to ask for a fork and spoon.

As you proceed through the meal, the empty food containers can be stacked neatly on the table and removed by the service staff.

Chinese tea flows freely during a *tim sum* lunch and the atmosphere is bustling and informal.

SET MEAL Many Chinese eating places offer set lunches and dinners, and these are representative of typical Chinese meals.

For all meals, the style of service will depend

on where and what you choose to eat.

Usually, your order will be served all at the same time, placed at the centre of the table, and shared amongst the diners, although some restaurants serve dishes in courses. You may help yourself to second helpings from the serving bowls. STYLE OF SERVICE

Do check if you are unsure of anything. Your Chinese host or the service staff will normally be most happy to enlighten you about their food.

When uncertain, many of us will try to do as we see others doing. This happened to a newly arrived foreign government trade officer, much to his regret. The local business community hosted a luncheon in his honour in a grand Chinese restaurant. Anxious to be a good guest, and happy to show his prowess with chopsticks, the gentleman happily ate as his hosts did. When they helped themselves to sliced green food and placed the slices in small bowls containing soya sauce, so did he. Whereas they were oblivious to the taste, the poor fellow took a mouthful of the green chillies and almost convulsed with the fiery taste! He coughed, gasped and had tears in his eyes from the unfamiliar chilli-hot taste! Looking back, he can laugh about the incident, but at the time he found it most embarrassing and his hosts felt apologetic that they had not thought to warn him of any tastes that he might not have been familiar with!

35

TEA

In many Chinese homes and workplaces there is a pot of hot Chinese tea constantly available. Padded containers are sometimes used to keep the pot of tea warm.

All the tea in the world originally came from China and, in the traditional way, tea-drinking is an art and an important part of Chinese culture.

Tea is drunk as an aid to digestion.

Chinese tea comes in a variety of flavours and is drunk without milk or sugar.

Green (unfermented) teas are highly thought of, such as the notable Dragon's Well (Longjing) varieties, also semi-green (partially fermented tea called Oolong) such as the well-known Iron Goddess of Mercy (Tie Guanyin). There are also red (fully fermented) teas (called 'black' tea in English) like the famous Keemun(Qimen), and flower teas including Jasmine (Moli) and Chrysanthemum (Juhua). Chrysanthemum is the only Chinese tea with added sugar.

Morning tea is usually a simple family matter, but afternoon tea may be more elaborate with, perhaps, savoury biscuits or cakes.

When drinking Chinese tea throughout a meal, it is usual to top up others' cups before attending to one's own cup.

Each time Chinese tea is poured for you, you thank the person pouring. It is most discourteous not to drink some tea (just a

few sips will do) each time it is served.

INDICATING THANKS WHEN SERVED TEA

You may observe Chinese gentlemen tapping the first two fingers of the right hand on the table when being served tea. This simply means "Thank you" and evolved during the Qing dynasty. Emperor Qian Long, travelling incognito, poured tea for fellow drinkers, including his body guard, in a tea house. The bodyguard, unable to bow in thanks without revealing his master's identity, tapped the table with his right index and middle fingers in the form of a bow, as a mark of respect.

REQUESTING MORE TEA

If, in a Chinese restaurant, you want your teapot refilled, simply tilt the lid and the waiter will take care of it. There is an interesting story of how this custom arose. A scholar brought his favourite pet bird with him to a teahouse one winter's day and, after finishing his pot of tea, placed the bird in the covered tea pot to keep warm. A waiter, not realising what the scholar had

done, refilled the pot with hot tea and killed the poor bird. From then on, it was said, to indicate that you wanted to have your teapot refilled, you had to remove the lid as a sign that the pot was indeed empty.

Chinese teacups do not have handles and can be hot to hold. The correct way is to hold the cup in the right hand by placing the thumb and index finger on opposite sides of the top rim and the small finger on the edge of the base of the cup. Lifting the cup with both hands (the right index finger and thumb holding the top rim and the left hand simply supporting the underneath of the cup) is most courteous.

When glasses are used instead of cups, the glass is held in the right hand near the rim, with the fingers of the left hand supporting the underneath of the glass.

If you do not want any more to drink, simply place your hand over your cup or glass when the drink is offered, or leave the cup almost full of tea.

PLACING YOUR ORDER

Chinese eating places featuring different styles of cooking abound.

Rice *(fan)*, and noodles *(mian)*, are always on the menu and are basic staple food. Northern Chinese cuisine also offers buns *(mantou)* as a staple food.

It is usual to order rice or noodles and, for an everyday Chinese meal, as many dishes (small, medium or large portions, depending on the number of diners) as there are persons. More can be ordered as the meal progresses, if necessary.

A meal should include at least one poultry dish, one meat and one fish dish, and always soup and vegetables. For a small party fewer dishes may be ordered.

There should ideally be soft and crisp foods, spicy and bland, delicate and robust flavours. Also pale and rich colours and always a green vegetable. Seasonal vegetables can be ordered, either stir-fried with meat, with oyster sauce or simply stir-fried with a little oil for the enjoyment of their natural flavours.

A variety of sweet desserts is common in Chinese cuisine. For examples, see the section on Food, Glorious Food! Fresh fruit is also often available.

Remember that the dishes are shared amongst the diners. Each person helps himself from the various central dishes as and when wished throughout the meal.

If you are eating alone, there are many one-dish meals to choose from, such as Yangzhou Fried Rice, Hainanese Chicken Rice, claypot rice, plus set meals. There are also noodle dishes such as Hokkien Mee (fried yellow noodles with seafood, meat, vegetables and a thick sauce), Teochew Kway Teow (white flat noodles with a touch of yellow noodles, fried with egg, Chinese sausage, fish cake, clams, lard and chilli sauce), Cantonese Korn Lo Meen (thin yellow noodles, boiled and served dry with green leafy vegetable, barbecued pork and special sauce and usually accompanied by a side serving of Wantan — pork dumpling soup), and vegetarian noodles.

It should be noted that some Chinese do not eat beef, as cattle are respected for their service to mankind. Many Buddhists do not eat meat on the first and 15th days of each lunar month, as a sign of compassion. Some Chinese are strictly vegetarian, including Buddhist monks and nuns.

When you are entertaining Chinese guests, whether at home or in a restaurant, be sure and check beforehand that your choice of food is acceptable to your guests, simply by asking them. Similarly, as a guest, you should inform your host beforehand of any dietary restrictions you may have.

If you are ordering a Chinese vegetarian meal, the same general guidelines apply to the number of dishes as for a non-vegetarian Chinese meal. Some of the dishes are made to resemble meat, simply to provide a change in the diet, using soya bean curd and gluten, among other ingredients. Authentic Chinese vegetarian dishes do not include garlic and members of the onion family, as they are reckoned to be similar to meat because of their strong flavour.

It is usual to order three vegetable dishes (including soya bean curd), one of which should be dry and the other two with sauces, plus soup and noodles or rice for a vegetarian meal. The choice is great — mushrooms, corn, peas, cabbage, carrots, nuts. Remember that the dishes are shared amongst the diners. COMPOSITION OF A VEGETARIAN MEAL

Vegetarian desserts include those made from nuts, soya bean curd and fruit. Cakes and pastries (made without eggs) are popular.

At a Chinese restaurant, the host will do the ordering. If it is an informal meal, you should decide amongst yourselves which dishes to order, and one person should place the order with the waiter. ORDERING FOOD

If you do not have a Chinese friend to assist you with any of the meals, then ask the waiter for advice on ordering.

For gastronomic delights, see the section on Food, Glorious Food!

ORDERING DRINKS

Chinese tea is the usual drink to be served throughout a Chinese meal and also ends the meal. It is drunk without milk or sugar. TEA

41

Soft drinks and beer are usually available and brandy is a popular dinner drink for gentlemen. Chinese businessmen, in particular, are partial to drinking cognac, neat or with water, by the tumblerful. Some prefer it with ice. To the Chinese, cognac has rejuvenating powers and tales abound of copious amounts being downed in an evening. Huge cognac sales in Singapore, Hong Kong, Malaysia and Thailand are fabled — leaving importers gasping with delight.

If you want an authentic Chinese alcoholic beverage, try Chinese rice or sorghum wine *(jiu)*. Note that *'jiu'*, the Chinese word for 'wine', applies to all alcoholic drinks — wine, liquor or spirit. Therefore be specific if you want traditional Chinese wine.

The making of Chinese *jiu*, goes back as far as 2000 B.C. Rice grains and sorghum are the main ingredients and Chinese *jiu*, vary in colour from clear to pale yellow to dark brown. Some are sweet and rich and some are very strong. *Shaoxing jiu* and *bai jiu* are well-known types.

Shaoxing jiu is made with water drawn from Jing Lake, Shaoxing, in Zhejiang Province of China. The wine is kept in earthenware jars to age at least one year before being put on sale, although many wines are matured for more than five years. The main ingredients of *Shaoxing* wine are glutinous rice, wheat, a little barley and yeast. Some of the most well-known brands are Hong Zhuangyuan (Red Scholar), Zhu Ye Qing (Bamboo Green) and Huadiao (Carved Flower).

Bai jiu is one of the most well-known sorghum spirits. Sorghum is a cereal grain plant that is used in a variety of ways, including making syrup, flour and alcoholic beverages. It is said that there are more than 700 makes of sorghum spirits. The ingredients are quite numerous, in fact anything that contains starch and sugar, such as sorghum, barley, corn, millet and potatoes, can be used.

Bai jiu is made throughout China — in the north, gluten-free sorghum is used; and in the south, glutinous sorghum. The spirits have a fragrant flavour and are reputed to promote good health.

Fen jiu, short for *Shanxifenyang jiu*, is one of the many *bai jiu* family. *Fen jiu* owes its uniqueness to the water used from a tributary of the Yellow River. *Maotai*, another *bai jiu*, is named after the town Maotai in the County of Renhua in the province of Guizhou. Long aging and traditional brewing give *maotai* its characteristically distinctive bouquet. It is said that *maotai* is comparable to French brandy. Its alcoholic strength is stronger than pure vodka!

Chinese rice wine is best when it is warmed before drinking, by standing the wine container in a pot of hot water, similar to the serving of Japanese *sake*. Sorghum spirits are served warm in cold climates and at room temperature in hot weather.

HOLDING
A WINE CUP

Jiu is served in small porcelain cups. The cup is held in the right hand with the thumb and index finger on the opposite sides of the top rim and the small finger on the base of the cup. To lift the cup with both hands is courteous — the left hand simply supporting the underneath of the cup.

When eating Chinese food, normally only one type of Chinese wine is served with the meal, and the choice depends on the host's liking.

RICE WINE
COCKTAILS

A trend in Hong Kong and Taiwan is to make cocktails using *bai jiu* as a base. The *bai jiu* is mixed with mineral water, soda water, lemon juice or similar, together with crushed ice. *Shaoxing jiu* can be served with a salted plum, making it taste much like sweet sherry.

GRAPE WINE

Wine-making using grapes is a relatively new industry in China, although the art was introduced during the Han Dynasty (206 B.C. – A.D. 220). Both red and white wines are made, but they do not have the same popularity in China as rice wines and sorghum spirits.

When choosing wine made from grapes to accompany Chinese meals, dry, or medium-dry, crisp wines are generally recommended, white or red depending on the food ordered and the host's preference.

White wines are normally served chilled and red wines at room temperature.

Ice cubes are often placed in glasses of beer as the beer is not always chilled — something strange to many foreigners!

BEER WITH ICE

When toasting during a Chinese meal, any drink is acceptable, whether it be brandy, tea or a soft drink. The glass or cup is held in both hands and should be held up high. Toasting is done to the long drawn-out shouts of *"Yam Seng"* (Cantonese, drink for success).

TOASTING

When drinking brandy or wine from a glass tumbler, the tumbler is held in the right hand with the left hand underneath the tumbler.

Table Etiquette

Now that the selection of the dishes has been taken care of, the actual eating and etiquette come into play. It is good if one has some understanding of the practices involved as one will then be able to more fully appreciate the joys of Chinese cuisine, although the whole idea is to enjoy the food! Chinese meals are generally friendly, relaxed and noisy affairs with much chattering and discussion.

When eating in the Chinese way, all the dishes are laid out in the centre of the table.

NUTS AND PICKLES

At a restaurant, nuts and pickles are usually already on the table when guests arrive. They should be eaten with chopsticks, but since it takes considerable skill to pick up nuts with chopsticks, fingers may be used. The nuts and pickles are not complimentary — you pay for them whether or not they are eaten!

CONDIMENTS

Small bottles or dishes of condiments such as chilli sauce, plum sauce, soya sauce and vinegar are normally available on tables.

Soya sauce, used as a flavouring in lieu of salt, is served in a small individual dish. Using your utensils, food may be gently dipped in the sauce before eating. When dipping food in common condiments, such as chilli sauce and pepper, be sure to only place the untouched section of food into the condiments, for hygienic reasons, and do not deposit rice from your chopsticks in the condiments.

If more sauce or condiments are required, you may request them from the waiter.

HAND TOWEL

Diners are often given damp hand towels before and after a Chinese meal, with which to wipe hands and mouth. After use, the soiled section is folded inwards and the towel is placed casually on the table next to your setting.

TOAST BY HOST & INVITATION TO BEGIN EATING

Before eating, whether at home or in a restaurant, it is usual for the Chinese host to raise his glass or cup and toast the guest-of-honour (if there is one) and all present will then do likewise, and take a sip of their drinks. Then, the host will take up his chopsticks, gesture towards the food, and invite guests to help themselves, saying, "*Ching*" ('please', implying help yourselves). Once this is done, everyone may begin eating. At banquets with many tables, where there will not be a host at each table, anyone may perform the courtesy of inviting one-and-all to begin eating.

Younger Chinese will always invite their elders at the table to eat before they themselves begin eating, perhaps with, *"Chi fan"* (literally, 'eat rice'). If you are greeted in such a way, you can simply reply with, "Let's eat".

INVITING ELDERS TO BEGIN EATING

The guest-of-honour should serve himself first, after being invited to do so by the host. Other guests then help themselves and the host serves himself last.

GUEST-OF-HONOUR TO BEGIN

You should note that to be served with a morsel of food from the Chinese host's chopsticks is a compliment, so do eat that particular piece of food even if it is not to your liking.

If the rice is served in a central bowl, just fill your individual rice bowl with rice using the serving spoon. Rice is eaten directly from the individual rice bowl using chopsticks. To begin eating, the rice bowl is picked up first, then the chopsticks. The most acceptable way to hold a rice bowl is to pick it up with the left hand, with the four fingers underneath the bowl and the thumb resting lightly on the top rim. To pick up the rice bowl with the left hand only, tilt the bowl away from you by pushing the rim with your thumb, then slip your fingers under the bowl.

HOLDING A RICE BOWL

The bowl is held in one hand at chin level, or at a level which is comfortable. Whilst eating rice, the edge of the bowl rests on the lower lip and the chopsticks do the moving, either pushing or shovelling the

EATING RICE FROM A BOWL

food into the mouth. The chopsticks ends (eating ends) are together, but not necessarily touching each other, when eating rice in this way.

Other food is taken from the central dishes onto your individual plate, using the serving spoon or your own chopsticks, and then transferred to the mouth or to the rice bowl. The food can be eaten with rice or eaten separately.

With a little practise, chopsticks are easy to manipulate. If it proves really difficult, then request a plate and a fork and spoon. Having seen, on a number of occasions, Westerners slowly and labouriously eating

rice with a fork, I feel it is worth mentioning here that, when eating Chinese food with a fork and spoon, the rice is eaten from the spoon. Grains of rice and fork tines are not good partners! In the Asian way, the fork is held with the inner curved side facing the user and is used to push food onto the spoon. The edge of the spoon can be used to cut food or separate meat from bones.

USING CHOPSTICKS

Chopsticks are Chinese eating utensils consisting of a pair of slim sticks, approximately 22 – 25 centimetres long, often made of bamboo, plastic or ivory, with the top thicker than the bottom (eating) ends which are rounded and narrow.

To use chopsticks, pick up the chopsticks

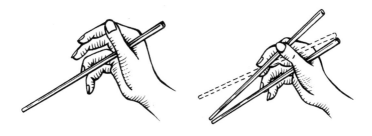

two-thirds way up (nearer to the top han-
dling ends) as though picking up a pen to
write. They must be level — simply tap the
eating ends on the table. It is impolite to tap
the ends of chopsticks elsewhere other than
on the table. The chopsticks can be held
with one stick wedged in the base of the
thumb and index finger, and resting on the
tip of the ring finger. The other stick is held
like a pencil on top of the first chopstick. The
thumb, index and middle fingers should be
relaxed and the chopsticks held by the
finger tips.The top chopstick does the work,
with the other chopstick held stationary as a
base. It works for me!

Chopsticks are normally arranged on the
table at a right angle to your body. Chopsticks must be placed on the chopsticks-rest,
or on the individual soya sauce dish, when
they are not in use during a meal, with the
eating ends of the sticks resting on the
chopsticks-rest or dish and the other ends
on the table. In the absence of a chopsticks-

PLACEMENT OF
CHOPSTICKS

rest or soya sauce dish, the chopsticks may be placed neatly across the rice bowl, at a slight angle to you. When you are eating from a dinner plate (for instance, with noodles), the chopsticks can either rest neatly on the side of your plate, or be placed with the eating ends of the chopsticks on your plate and the other ends on the table.

OFFERING FOOD TO ANOTHER WITH YOUR CHOPSTICKS

If you are offering food to another person using your own chopsticks, turn the chopsticks around and use the thicker (clean) ends, for hygienic purposes. Westerners, in particular, are surprised when food is served to them from another's utensils, often to the detriment of their appetite for an otherwise delicious meal.

TABOOS WITH CHOPSTICKS

There are a few 'rules' to observe when using chopsticks. Chinese superstition has it that if chopsticks are dropped, it is a sign of bad luck. Chopsticks must not be stuck upright in a bowl of rice as that resembles joss-sticks in an urn at an altar. Chopsticks must not be crossed one over the other. They must not be used for gesticulating or pointing, except when gesturing to invite guests to begin eating. They also should not be sucked on.

BEGIN BY EATING RICE

When rice is served at the same time as other food, one should begin the meal by eating one or two mouthfuls of rice, as rice is the principal food.

EATING RICE WITH OTHER FOOD

It is usual to eat one type of food at one mouthful, to fully appreciate the taste. Rice

52

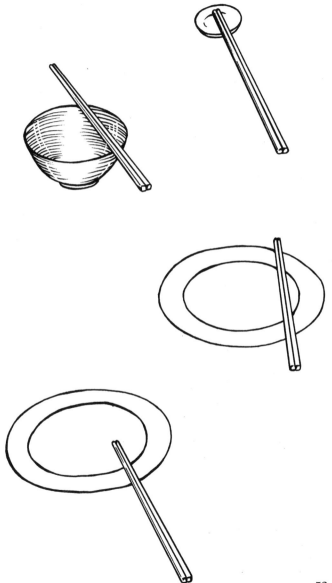

should be alternated with other food.

Eating is done quietly, chewing with the mouth closed, although a little noise is in order. Gentle burping by Chinese is a sign of appreciation of the food consumed.

Elbows do not belong on the table.

SERVING YOURSELF

Serving dishes of food are often placed on a turn-table on the table enabling all present to help themselves. When serving yourself, do not lift the serving dish up, it remains on the turn-table or table. Your own individual plate also remains on the table, although it may be moved nearer to the serving dish, and food is transferred from one to the other with a serving spoon.

PASSING A SERVING DISH

If there is no turn-table, the dishes from the opposite sides of the table may be exchanged so that everyone can easily help themselves to the different dishes.

If a serving spoon is not provided, you should use your own chopsticks and/or spoon to help yourself, taking care not to touch food other than that which you wish to consume. Or you may request a serving spoon if in a restaurant.

When serving yourself with solid food from central serving bowls, the food is placed onto your individual plate. If the food is saucy, it is placed directly into your rice bowl.

Do not take the biggest piece of food on the serving plate and do not take the last piece of food, unless you are urged to do so repeatedly. Also, do not reach over another's chopsticks when helping yourself. Always take the food nearest to you on the serving dish.

When offered a second helping, it is good manners to refuse at first, then, after urging by the host, to accept if you wish to.

SECOND HELPING

There are many courses, usually eight or ten, to a formal Chinese meal, and one should endeavour to eat small portions from each course. It is impolite to refuse anything (unless due to dietary restrictions).

'TEN COURSE' DINNER

At a formal Chinese dinner, first a combination of appetisers, commonly called the 'cold dish', is served, after which the dishes include poultry, thick soup, prawns, vegetables and pork (though not necessarily in that order). Fish is served towards the end of the meal, followed by a staple such as noodles or fried rice. Dessert and Chinese tea complete the meal.

FORMAL ORDER OF COURSES

Fish should always be served with the head pointing towards the guest-of-honour, as should poultry and suckling pig.

Dishes are served one at a time at a formal meal and not altogether. Serving dishes remain on the table for a short while if food remains on them, and they are moved to the left when the next dish is served. Your table server will ask if a dish of food, apparently finished with, may be removed.

FORMAL STYLE OF SERVICE

At a Chinese family meal at home, several dishes of food and a soup tureen will be

A HOME-COOKED MEAL

placed in the centre of the table and each person will have a bowl or plate of rice. When eating a home-cooked Chinese meal, serve yourself small portions from the dishes as and when you please. Soup may be drunk throughout the meal. Your host will be complimented if a second helping of rice is asked for.

PAYING COMPLIMENTS ON FOOD SERVED

The Chinese love food and they often express praise when a dish is served, commenting on the appearance and then the taste. This praise will endear the guest to the host, as a Chinese host always takes a lot of care and thought in the choice of food served. Whether you are a guest at home or in a restaurant, praise is appreciated, but the host will insist that the meal is a simple one even if the most extravagant meal has been served.

FINISHING A MEAL

It is good etiquette at a Chinese meal to empty one's rice bowl by eating all the rice.

UTENSILS

Upon finishing a meal, chopsticks are placed together to the right side of your rice bowl, either resting on the chopsticks-rest or on the table at right angles to you. They should not be placed on the rice bowl.

With a Western setting, the fork and spoon are placed side by side on the individual dinner plate, with the handles towards the diner.

TOOTHPICK

A toothpick is commonly used at the end of a Chinese meal, using the right hand, with the left hand held over the mouth as a form of courtesy.

After a meal it is customary to say, "*Xie xie*" (thank you) to the Chinese host, and the host will reply with, "Don't mention it", or a similar remark.

The Chinese are relatively fast eaters and once a formal meal at a restaurant is finished, there is no lingering, everyone takes off! However, as a dinner guest at home, it is appropriate to stay for a short time after the meal before taking one's leave.

It is in order for you, as the one paying the restaurant bill, to request that any food remaining on the serving dishes after the meal has ended, be suitably packed for you to take home (*da bao*). You have paid for the food, and it makes a nice lunch for the morrow!

Remember when you are entertaining Chinese friends, that an even number of courses should be served. Also, an even number of persons is preferred, for good luck. Businessmen in particular should be aware of this.

SPECIFIC CHINESE FOOD
Some food may prove to be a little difficult to eat for the uninitiated.

The large claws of crabs are normally cracked in the kitchen before being served, making for easier eating. Sometimes nutcrackers are provided to help one along. The fingers are used to pull the shell apart

57

and the crab meat is extracted either with the fingers or with a fork.

After extracting the crab meat from the claws, the meat is eaten with the accompanying sauce (if there is sauce), using a fork or using a chunk of bread (if served) as a pusher or scoop. With the fingers, the small claws are pulled from the body of the crab, then broken and the broken ends are sucked in the mouth to savour the meat. The body is broken to expose the flesh, then held in one hand and taken to the mouth. The flesh is eaten and more shell is broken off to expose the flesh. Small pieces of shell are bound to find their way into the diner's mouth, and these are extracted discreetly with the fingers of the other hand. Damp towels, or finger-bowls with water or tea and fresh limes, are provided for this particular dish.

PRAWN   If you have an aversion to shelling cooked prawns, then check with the waiter before ordering as to whether they are served shelled. When it is necessary to shell the cooked prawns at the table, begin by removing the head of the crustacean with your fingers. Next remove part of the body shell and tail by pulling away the tail. Finally, remove the remaining shell and legs.

Prawns are taken and shelled one at a time, as you wish to eat them. The prawn is then eaten with your fingers.

Shells are placed on your plate, or on a

plate provided for such discarded items, or neatly on the table. Damp towels, or finger bowls with water or tea and fresh limes, are always available for soiled fingers.

SOUP

At a Chinese meal, soup is served in one central soup tureen, with a soup ladle.

SOUP

Soup is served and consumed as part of the main meal for the Chinese. Thick soup may be served as a second or third course at a formal Chinese dinner, while light soup is often served later, before the noodle or rice dishes. This often amuses Westerners, who are jokingly told that they are beginning the meal all over again!

SOUP SERVED AS PART OF A MAIN MEAL

In most Chinese restaurants, the serving staff proportion the soup into the individual soup bowls from the central tureen.

AT RESTAURANTS

At home, one helps oneself, by using the soup ladle and serving the soup from the tureen into the individual soup bowl.

AT HOME

The soup can then be consumed throughout the meal as one wishes.

When a soup bowl is not provided, you use your rice bowl for soup, at the end of the meal.

Soup is consumed with a spoon, with the spoon scooping towards the diner. The soup bowl is tilted towards the diner, where necessary, with it remaining on the table.

STYLE OF DRINKING SOUP

Chopsticks may be used to eat solid food from the soup bowl.

SOLID FOOD IN SOUP

The spoon remains in the soup bowl upon finishing the soup, the handle towards the diner.

A container of black or red vinegar is provided when shark's fin soup is served, for seasoning the soup as preferred. Some like to add a little brandy.

BONES

Any bones and other inedible foodstuff should be placed on the table beside your setting or on your small individual plate. In fine Chinese restaurants, the soiled plate will be cleared and a clean plate provided from time to time.

REMOVING BONES FROM MOUTH

Where possible, remove bones and shells from your mouth using chopsticks, though if this proves difficult then your fingers may be used in a delicate fashion.

SERVIETTES / TABLE NAPKINS

Serviettes, or table napkins, are not always used when eating Chinese food, as damp hand-towels are preferred.

USING A TABLE NAPKIN

If a table napkin is provided, it should be kept on the diner's lap except when being used to gently wipe hands and mouth.

In some restaurants, the table napkins are placed on the table as place-mats by waiters, for the dessert course, as the table-cloth is often soiled by that stage of the meal.

After a meal, the soiled section is folded inwards and the table napkin is placed casually on the table next to your setting.

After using a damp hand-towel, the soiled section is folded inwards and the towel is placed casually on the table next to your setting, and removed by service staff. USING A DAMP HAND TOWEL

When a damp paper towel in a plastic wrapper is offered for finger wiping, it should be placed neatly near your bowl or plate after use. The loud 'popping' of the package when opening the wrapper to remove the towel is fun, but not considered refined! PAPER TOWEL IN A PLASTIC WRAPPER

BUFFET

Chinese meals are not traditionally served buffet style, but hotel restaurants may have buffets featuring Chinese food, or hosts entertaining at home may serve a selection of Chinese dishes buffet style. When eating in such a manner, you gently help yourself to food from the buffet table, throughout the meal, and return to your table to eat. BUFFET

When food is presented in a small round bamboo container, you help yourself to one or two pieces of food from the container. Do not take the bamboo container, or any container, to your table.

BUSINESS

Business is uppermost on the minds of Chinese, therefore every opportunity to promote business contacts is taken, especially BUSINESS over a meal.

Never assume that a spouse is included in an invitation, check with the office concerned if you are unsure.

When giving and receiving a business card in the Chinese way, two hands must be used. The card is handed over so that the recipient can read it as given to him. A bow, or nod of the head, indicates good business etiquette when giving and receiving a card.

I observed a situation where a non-Asian businessman unceremoniously thrust his business card at an Asian gentleman, using his left hand only, the card at an angle and the printing facing away from the recipient. But being inscrutable, there was no obvious embarrassment, except for observers. Whether coincidental or not, the business deal fell through.

Business is not discussed until after pleasantries have been disposed of, in fact, sometimes never at all. This is because Chinese business meals are public relations exercises designed to impress guests and establish contacts. Thus, a host never stints. The restaurant should be one that the host is familiar with, and the menu should be chosen in advance in order that the host appears well-prepared and no problem arises.

Chinese guests at a business meal may make a show at offering to pay the bill at the end of the meal. Be prepared, as a guest will

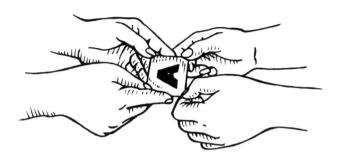

actually pay given the slightest opportunity. This move is in accordance with the philosophy of a business meal — he who pays scores points in public relations and secures a psychological obligation. Therefore this fighting over the bill is a ritual to traditional Chinese businessmen.

Festive Fare

LUNAR
NEW YEAR

The Lunar New Year celebrations last for 15 days, commencing on the first month of the lunar calendar (January or February), with the first day being the most important day in the year.

There are many traditions and customs associated with this festival, but as long as one appreciates that family ties are paramount and that this is *the* most important Chinese festival, then enjoyment is bound to follow.

DAYS FOR NEW
YEAR VISITS

The first and second days of the New Year are popular days for visiting older and respected relatives and friends. The third day is not a day for visiting, as it is believed that quarrels may take place. There is a superstition that if an unmarried girl ventures out on the third day, she will not find a husband.

DECORATION

Pussy willows, colourful flowers, pots of kumquats and red banners are in evidence, and homes and other buildings are made spick and span. These preparations begin well in advance. Household chores such as sweeping, dusting and washing are not carried out on New Year's Day, for fear of brushing away good luck.

On New Year's Eve, dinner is a family affair of great importance when family ties are strengthened. To be invited to this meal is a great honour.

FAMILY REUNION DINNER

Chinese sausages, waxed ducks, fresh fish, dried oysters and dried mushrooms will be seen on festive tables. Also traditionally eaten by the various dialect groups are noodles (for longevity), steamboat (where a variety of seafood, meat and vegetables is cooked in a communal hotpot), leeks (to ensure that there is plenty of money to count in the coming year), meat balls (round in shape signifying completeness), a black hair-like sea moss called *fa cai* or *fatt choy* in Cantonese (for prosperity) and yam dumplings, known as abacus beads (symbolising the counting of blessings in the year ahead), served with syrup. Trevally is an auspicious dish, as the fish spawn during the New Year season and the rich roe symbolises wealth and plenty.

FESTIVE FARE

Traditional snacks enjoyed during the New Year celebrations are groundnuts, sweets, chocolate 'coins' wrapped in gold foil, and a variety of traditional biscuits.

Favoured drinks are Chinese tea with red dates, orange-flavoured drinks and cognac.

Even when visiting a host of friends, it is

impolite to refuse food and drink at this auspicious time of year. Keep smiling and eating, and diet later!

FESTIVE GIFT

Nian gao (phonetically, sticky cake or new year cake) is a sweet, round, golden-brown cake made of sugar and glutinous rice, that implies *Nian Nian Gao Sheng* – rising higher every year. It is popular as a New Year gift for relatives, friends and businessmen. This sticky cake keeps well and slices can be steamed, or dipped into beaten egg and fried, before eating.

PRESENTING MANDARINS

Symbolising good luck, because of their shape and colour, and because the Cantonese pronunciation for this fruit is *'gum'*, which is similar in sound to 'gold', mandarins will be seen in abundance during this festive season. It is customary when visiting your Chinese friends to present an even number of the fruit (two is common) to your host, using both hands, with the wish,

SPOKEN GREETING

"*Gong Xi Fa Cai*" (a wish for prosperity), or "*Kong Hei Fatt Choy*" in Cantonese, or, more simply, "Happy New Year". A good host will reciprocate before you take your leave.

MONETARY GIFT OR RED PACKET

Hongbao, red envelopes containing money in an even number, are given to children and unmarried persons as good luck gifts by married relatives and friends during the New Year celebrations. It is considered ill-mannered to open the envelopes in the presence of the givers. Remember to present an even amount; depending on one's familiarity with the person, a general guide would be between S$2 and S$10.

The ritual of tossing and eating Yu Sheng (raw fish) is traditionally carried out on the seventh day of the first lunar month of the Chinese New Year, which is observed as Everybody's Birthday.

'Yu', the Chinese word for 'fish', has a similar sound to the word meaning 'abundance'. Fish are therefore looked upon as symbols of wealth and abundance. Their swift movements indicate freedom and lack of restriction, a sense of liveliness, which conjures up a picture of prosperity and expansion, especially in business. Fish normally swim in schools, thereby signifying harmony. *'Sheng'* is similar in sound to the word meaning 'life'. *'Yu Sheng'*, literally translated, is 'fish raw'.

Phonetically, when the words *'yu sheng'* are reversed, one gets a similar sound to the term for 'business'.

The Cantonese and the Teochew versions of this traditional dish are the most commonly served. They both feature finely sliced raw fish and a variety of sliced raw vegetables, served with sweet sauce and spices. The latter version is usually served in thicker slices than the former, and with less vegetables, with plum sauce as a dip. The fish and vegetables are often served separately.

For the Cantonese-style Yu Sheng, it is

RAW FISH

TEOCHEW
RAW FISH

CANTONESE
RAW FISH

usual to combine the fish, vegetables, sauce and spices together in one central dish.

STYLE OF SERVICE

At a restaurant, the waiter will bring the Yu Sheng ingredients and prepare the dish in a central plate at the table. Groups of businessmen, friends or family members, using chopsticks, mix the many ingredients of this raw fish dish with great relish, tossing the ingredients high up to the happy shouts of, *"Lo hei"* (in Cantonese), meaning to "raise up wealth".

Yu Sheng is traditionally served with rice porridge. Dried scallops and fish or chicken are often cooked in the porridge.

Festivities continue throughout the 15 days, with different dialect groups observing age-old traditions on various days.

The New Year celebrations draw to a close on the 15th night, *Yuan Xiao* (also known as *Chap Goh Mei*), of the new moon, with family feasts and activities. Red lanterns are the usual decorations.

DRAGON BOAT FESTIVAL

The Dragon Boat Festival is celebrated by the Chinese on the fifth day of the fifth month of the Lunar calendar (in June) to commemorate the death of the poet, Qu Yuan, of the Warring States period. Qu Yuan, in protest against anomalies in the government, committed suicide by throwing himself into the Mi-lo River. Fishermen in boats tried unsuccessfully to save him, and then threw rice dumplings into the river for his soul. Another version of this is that the fishermen threw the dumplings into the river for the fish so that they would not eat Qu Yuan's body.

Dragon boats, signifying the fishermen's boats, are raced and this event adds colour, excitement and noise to this festival.

Pyramid-shaped steamed glutinous rice dumplings wrapped in leaves and tied securely, are exchanged between relatives and friends and eaten. Popular types of dumplings available include the Hokkien version with a savoury filling of pork and dried prawns, wrapped in bamboo leaves, and the Nonya version with its sweetened pork filling, wrapped in pandanus leaves. The Cantonese version, filled with streaky-pork, mushrooms and chestnuts, is wrapped in lotus leaves.

The leaves must be opened up properly (fingers may be used) before commencing eating the dumpling straight off the leaves. The dumpling is eaten either with chopsticks or a fork. Upon finishing, the leaves are left on your plate or the table.

These dumplings are sold in some places throughout the year, but in abundance during the festive period.

The Mooncake Festival is celebrated on the fifteenth day of the eighth month of the Chinese calendar (September or October), when children parade in the evening with colourful and fanciful lighted lanterns.

There are many romantic stories, all focusing on the moon, associated with this festival.

One popular story tells of how secret messages were placed in mooncakes, to be distributed amongst the Chinese who were planning action against Mongolian rule during the Ming Dynasty. To signal the start of the action, lanterns were lit.

Another legend tells of the beautiful lady in the moon, Chang-E, who saved her people from the tyrannical rule of her husband Hou Yi, who had stolen the elixir of life. Chang-E did this by drinking the elixir and floating to the moon. She is today worshipped by many young girls during this festival.

This festival is also known as the Mid-Autumn Festival and in China it is a time of relaxation for farmers after the harvest. The moon is believed to be at its brightest for the occasion. It is also a popular month for weddings!

If you join your Chinese friends at home, you will no doubt be served with the traditional fare of mooncakes, pomelos, groundnuts, yams and Chinese tea. Sweets wrapped in pink paper are also popular, as are wheat flour cakes in fancy shapes nestled in little plastic baskets. There are also *ling ge*, hard, black nuts, shaped like a bull's head complete with sharp horns. They are cracked open so that the white, crunchy flesh can be enjoyed.

Mooncakes are small and round, or oval,

FESTIVE FARE

MOONCAKES

not only to resemble the moon, but also because the circular shape signifies completeness.

Popular types of mooncakes are the Cantonese-style with their thin golden brown pastry crust, and the Teochew-style with light, flaky pastry.

Favourite sweet fillings include solid pastes of red bean, black bean, mung bean, and the ever popular lotus seed paste with melon seeds. In the Teochew way the fillings are liberally mixed with lard.

Salted duck's-egg yolks are often added to the sweet fillings of Cantonese-style mooncakes, and are considered delicacies. The best quality Cantonese mooncakes contain four egg yolks, so that when the mooncakes are quartered, each piece will have a whole egg yolk.

Cantonese-style savoury fillings include ham, bacon, nuts and spices.

Be warned, mooncakes are very rich. Don't do as my Australian friend did and take a bite from a whole cake — by the end of the cake his teeth were practically standing on edge! Using a knife, a small wedge should be cut from the mooncake, which will be served on a central plate, then eaten using fingers. Chinese tea is usually served to counteract the richness.

Items such as mooncakes and pomelos are given in pairs or even numbers when presented as gifts.

FESTIVE GIFT

Food, Glorious Food!

Chinese food is, justifiably, one of the world's great cuisines.

The staple food for southern Chinese is rice *(fan)*, while for northern Chinese it is noodles *(mian)* or buns *(mantou)* made from wheat.

STAPLE FOOD

The most popular meat for the Chinese is pork, including Char Siew (barbecued pork) and roast pork. Roast suckling pig is a favourite dish. Pigs' intestines and other viscera are also considered great food.

POPULAR CHOICES

Chicken is also a popular item, with the wings and drumsticks preferred to other parts. Fish is an important item in the diet, especially fresh steamed fish. Soya bean products are served at almost every meal, in one form or another.

Lamb is not a great favourite due to its strong aroma.

Desserts are not a necessity at a Chinese meal, though fresh fruit is popular.

DESSERT

In Asia, a large variety of regional Chinese food can be found, from humble hawkers' stalls to elegant restaurants, so lovers of Chinese food have a real treat.

The five major styles of Chinese cooking are Cantonese, Hokkien, Hunan, Shantung/Beijing and Szechuan.

Here are some examples of the various styles. They do not represent complete meals; they are simply some of my own favourite Chinese dishes.

CANTONESE DISHES

Cantonese cuisine is perhaps the best-known Chinese food outside China, acclaimed for its variety of stir-fried delicacies. Seafood is an important item in the diet. *Dian xin* or *tim sum* is always a favourite.

Also, Sweet and Sour Pork: pork pieces cooked in a piquant sweet and sour sauce with onion, cucumber and pineapple. A Chinese dish created during the Qing dynasty to suit Western taste.

Yangzhou Fried Rice: with peas, prawns, roast pork and egg.

Korn Lo Meen: thin yellow noodles, boiled and served dry with green leafy vegetable, barbecued pork and special sauce and usually accompanied by a side serving of Wantan — pork dumpling soup.

Shark's Fin Soup: a thick soup, considered a delicacy, often flavoured with vinegar.

Sago and Melon dessert: pearl sago and melon, sweetened with rock sugar and coconut milk, served cold.

HOKKIEN DISHES

Hokkien style dishes, with their subtle flavours, feature fish, pork and clear soups, with red wine and soya sauce used in the cooking. Hokkien Popiah, or Bao Bing, (fresh spring roll) is justly famous.

Or try Hokkien Mee: fried flat yellow noodles with seafood, meat, vegetables and a thick sauce.

Khong Bak Bao: stewed streaky pork served with steamed buns.

Fried Oyster Omelette

Sparerib Soup: clear soup with pork spareribs, soya sauce, sugar, five-spice powder, vinegar and Chinese turnip.

Lychees with Almond Jelly.

HUNAN DISHES

Hunan cooking features subtle seasonings and pleasantly sharp tatstes, with sweet and sour fish being a fine example.

Also, Smoked Duck: with the golden skin rubbed with sesame oil.

Fish and Vegetable Broth: a clear soup.

Sweet and Sour Fish: carp, often fried, served with pungent, sweet, sauce made with garlic, oil, sugar and wine.

Pigeon in Bamboo Cups: steamed minced pigeon and water chestnuts, with a rich broth.

Waterchestnut with Sesame Seed: with crushed waterchestnuts, sweetened red bean paste and white sesame seeds.

SHANTUNG/BEIJING DISHES

Beijing is the home of the renowned Peking Duck and the cuisine includes dishes that are braised, fried and stewed, with delicate flavours emphasised. Garlic and spring onions are widely used.

Peking Duck: roast duck prized for its crisp golden skin. A piece of meat with skin is placed on a small pancake, together with spring onion and thick sweet plum sauce, to be folded over and eaten using fingers or chopsticks.

Bean Curd Soup: a clear soup with soya bean curd, Chinese mushrooms and pork.

Liver with Vegetables: stir-fried pig's liver with assorted vegetables, such as bamboo shoot, carrot and snow peas.

Five-spice Chicken: marinated and deep-fried.

Candied Apples: toffee-coated sliced apples, served hot, which are dipped in water at the table resulting in a crisp toffee coating.

SZECHUAN DISHES

Szechuan cooking features hot, spicy dishes with chillies, ginger, hot pepper, spring onions and sesame oil frequently used. Fungi are also favoured. If you like food with a pep, then this style is for you.

Pork with Fish Flavour: stir-fried diced pork with hot bean paste, wood ears (small, crinkled black fungi), water chestnuts and a piquant sauce.

Chicken with Dried Chillies: diced chicken sauteed with dried chillies and a spicy sauce.

Hot and Sour Soup: with pork or chicken, Chinese mushrooms, bamboo shoots, transparent vermicelli, ginger, tomato sauce, soya sauce, vinegar and egg.

Sweet Bean Pancakes: pancakes filled with a thick, sweet, red bean paste.

Other popular styles include the following, readily available, ones.

HAINANESE DISHES

In Hongkong, Singapore and Malaysia, Hainanese chefs prepare wonderful pork chop and chicken chop dishes, reminiscent of colonial style. Hainanese cooks have a special way with flavourings, as seen in their speciality, Chicken Rice.

Chicken Rice: tender pieces of boiled chicken served with rice cooked in chicken stock, a bowl of cabbage soup and condiments of chilli sauce, ginger sauce, soya sauce and fresh cucumber.

Hainanese Pork Chop: boneless pork chop, breadcrumbed and fried, served with gravy, peas and potatoes.

HAKKA DISHES

Hakka cooking is known as hearty, simple country style fare. A special flavour is imparted by glutinous rice wine. Vegetables and soya bean curd are favourite items, often stuffed with minced seafood, as in

Yong Tauhu (Niang Doufu).

Salt-baked Chicken: baked, covered in sea-salt.

Stuffed Bean Curd (Yong Tauhu): cakes of soya beancurd stuffed with minced seafood and served in various ways.

SHANGHAINESE DISHES

SHANGHAINESE

Shanghai dishes are rich and hearty, often salty and favouring thick sauces. Seafood is a popular item in the diet.

Shanghainese Hairy Crab: served with a traditional sauce of red vinegar with ginger slices.

Bird's Nest Soup: the celebrated and sweet dish, made from the nests of swifts.

TEOCHEW DISHES

TEOCHEW

Good, simple, hearty food is enjoyed by the Teochews, with the taste a little to the salty side. Braised goose and steamed fish are their specialities.

Braised Goose: in a rich stock.

Steamed fish: with pomfret and groupa being among the most popular

Fried Kway Teow: white flat noodles with a touch of yellow noodles, fried with egg, Chinese sausage, fish cake, clams, lard and chilli sauce.

TIM SUM SELECTION

TIM SUM

Steamed Prawn Dumpling (Har Kow): tiny, steamed, pleated, closed dumpling with translucent dough of tapioca flour and wheat starch.

Pork and Prawn Dumpling (Siew Mai): steamed dumpling shaped like a tiny open pot of food, with dough of glutinous flour, egg and cornflour.

Barbecued Pork Bun (Char Siew Bao): soft, steamed bun with diced barbecued pork filling, served warm.

OTHER FAVOURITES

Other Chinese favourites apart from rice, noodles and vegetables, include:

Popiah: a fresh — not fried — Spring Roll where everyone prepares their own roll at the table by adding ingredients, including a variety of cooked vegetables, pork, prawns, soya beancurd, chilli and sweet sauce, to an egg and rice flour *crepe*.

Steamboat: where everyone cooks fresh ingredients, including seafood, vegetables, soya beancurd and noodles, in a central pot of boiling soup stock on the table.

Pork Spare Ribs.

"Ching."
Eat and enjoy!

THE PERANAKANS

PERANAKAN
COMMUNITY
Within the Chinese community in Southeast Asia, there is a sub-culture with a delightfully rich and colourful heritage.

The Peranakans (*Baba* is the term for a male, *Nonya* for female) are originally people from Malacca, Penang, Singapore and Indonesia of Chinese fathers and Malay mothers, with subsequent generations marrying within their own unique community or into the Chinese community. They speak Baba Malay, a distinctive patois based on Malay and laced with Hokkien dialect. Their traditions are Chinese with Malay influences.

Peranakan etiquette combines both the Chinese and Malay styles of manners, and places great emphasis on genteel behaviour.

BELIEFS
Various religious beliefs are practised, but Chinese rites and rituals are predominant in the daily lives of the Peranakan people.

They are well-known for their artistic creativity, including fine needlework and culinary skills.

80

When visiting a traditional Peranakan home, one may be fortunate enough to see antique wooden furniture with intricate carvings sometimes inlaid with gold leaf or mother of pearl, and tables with marble tops. Family altars are often draped with richly embroidered colourful altar cloths during feast days.

PERANAKAN HOME DECOR

The older traditional Nonya can be seen wearing the Malay-style *sarong kebaya* – a colourful sarong with a long-sleeved blouse fashioned from lacy translucent material. A set of three brooches (*kerosang*) takes the place of buttons at the front of the blouse, and a silver belt and buckle might also be worn. Beautifully beaded slippers sometimes complete the outfit. More's the pity we don't see enough of these original outfits. Babas wear trousers and shirts rather than the traditional loose *baju* (shirt) and pyjama-like trousers.

TRADITIONAL DRESS

Traditional Baba weddings are not common these days. However, if you are invited to such a ceremony you will be enthralled by the heavy, colourful, embroidered wedding costumes worn by the groom and his bride.

MARRIAGE CEREMONY

At a wedding dinner, Jantong Pisang (a salad made with banana flower buds, coconut milk, prawns, chillies and lemon) is usually served and Hee Peow Soup (a rich soup with fish maw, fish balls, prawn balls and pork balls), as well as a large variety of rich and spicy dishes. Pineapple tarts and

AUSPICIOUS FARE

Love Letters or Kueh Blandah (crispy, rolled crepes) are also favourites.

BIRTHDAY

At a birthday party, Nasi Kunyit (glutinous rice cooked with saffron and coconut milk) is served. Mee Sua (thread-like wheat flour noodles) are also served, representing longevity. It is impolite for a guest to refuse these noodles, as the eating of them signifies the wish for a long life for the birthday celebrant.

FUNERAL

Funeral rites are similar to those of the Chinese. Simple food is served to visitors and, after the funeral, noodles are served for the purpose of wishing visitors long life.

HOME-COOKED MEAL

When invited home for a Nonya meal, the food is occasionally laid out on a long table (*tok panjang*) and eating may be in shifts, depending on how many persons are present. After one group has finished eating at the table, the plates are quickly cleared. Fresh food is added to the serving bowls, and the other guests are then invited to take their turn. The host-family members usually eat last.

TABLE SETTING

For a Nonya meal, the setting comprises a dinner plate with a fork to the left, a spoon to the right, and a soup bowl at the top right of the setting. Knives are not used as the food is served in bite-sized portions. Drinks are placed to the top right of each setting.

Antique nonya-ware, seen on tables for special occasions, is colourful and elegant.

ORDERING A PERANAKAN MEAL

Cooking is an art that Nonyas excel in and you should try some of their dishes to appreciate the marriage of Chinese ingredients with Malay spices. Peranakan food is rich and spicy. Soups are rich without being heavy and are mostly adapted from Chinese recipes. The staple food is boiled rice, accompanied by meat stews, poultry, fish and vegetables, all prepared in bite-size pieces.

A condiment called *sambal blachan* is always served with meals, prepared with chillies, dried shrimp paste and lime juice. Be warned, it is very hot. *Achar* (pickles) is another popular side dish.

Usually a Nonya meal will include a spicy dish with gravy, a mild dish with gravy and two dishes with little or no gravy. If soup, or a soupy dish, is eaten it is served in a Chinese-style bowl. Nonya food is shared amongst the diners. The meal is likely to end with a sweet dessert.

Previously, food was eaten with the fingers, but it is customary nowadays to use a setting of fork, spoon and dinner plate. Upon finishing the meal, the fork and spoon are placed side by side on one's dinner plate, with the handles towards the diner, Western style.

Fresh lime juice and barley water are popular drinks with a Nonya meal. Coffee is also popular, drunk with or without evapo-

CONDIMENTS

COMPOSITION OF MEAL

UTENSILS

DRINKS

rated or condensed milk, and sugar. Coffee beans from Malaysia as well as Indonesia are favoured.

PERANAKAN FARE

Nonya favourites to try are Ayam Buah Keluak (*'ayam'* is chicken and *'buah keluak'* is a large black nut from Indonesia with a soft, fragrant centre), and Ayam Sioh (chicken in tamarind sauce), Sayur Lodeh (a spicy vegetable dish), Babi Pong Teh (stewed pork), Assam Prawns (prawns in a spicy tamarind sauce) and Mee Siam (fried vermicelli with spicy gravy).

DESSERT

Nonya desserts include sweet, colourful cakes *(kueh)* made with rice flour and coconut milk. Other favourites are Gula Melaka (cold sago pudding with palm sugar syrup and coconut milk), Pulot Hitam (a thick porridge made of black glutinous rice, with palm sugar and coconut milk) and Pangat Pisang (bananas cooked in coconut milk with palm sugar). They make a sweet, cool finish to a hot, spicy meal.

EATING ALONE

If you are eating alone, there are one-dish meals available, such as Chicken Macaroni Soup, Mee Siam and Laksa (rice noodles in a rich, spicy soup).

Otak Otak is also a popular dish. Minced fish meat mixed with a spicy paste is placed securely in coconut leaves before being grilled. The leaves should be opened up fully, using fingers, before commencing eating. It is usual, in the Nonya way, at the table, to use a fork and spoon for this item.

Tropical Fruit

Fresh tropical fruit is plentiful in Asia, inexpensive and deliciously nutritious. Fruit can be bought in slices from vendors, bought singly or in bulk from markets and supermarkets and ordered in restaurants.

Just as kiwifruit may cause an Asian to decide against trying it, so durian or rambutan may cause a Westerner to back off, because of unfamiliarity. Having watched an Englishman trying unsuccessfully to cut open a durian a few words are appropriate here.

RAMBUTAN

The rambutan tree originated in Malaysia and the small fruit has a red hairy covering which easily pulls apart around the middle. Using your thumbs and fingers, break the fruit to expose the white, juicy pulp. The single central seed is not eaten.

Durian, considered the king of fruits, is spherical, football-size, has a thick, hard, spiky, greenish-yellow husk and an extremely strong aroma. The seller will pry the durian open along its nearly invisible wedges (there is an art to this) for the buyer, upon

DURIAN

request. Soft, juicy, creamy gold pulp around large brown seeds is found inside – the taste is one of a kind! Be warned, many establishments prohibit the fruit within their premises as the aroma tends to linger.

JACKFRUIT

Jackfruit, or nanka , is also a large fruit (up to 60 centimetres long) and it is usual to buy it in segments. The brownish-yellow, sticky flesh surrounding the seeds also has a distinctive aroma.

PINEAPPLE

Much more fragrant and sweet-tasting is the juicy, yellow pineapple, which, after having the outer greenish-brown, hard scaly skin removed, is cut into slices and sometimes dipped in salt before being eaten.

MANGOSTEEN

Also sweet and juicy are mangosteens. The delicate white segments are found in a round, smooth, thick, firm purple casing with red rind. The tennis-ball-size fruit should be squashed open gently in your palms. Take care as the juice stains clothes permanently.

DUKU / LANGSAT

The golf-ball-size duku and its cousins the langsat and duku-langsat, are also squashed open by using both palms or thumbs and index fingers. The golden-brown skin will reveal juicy segments of translucent flesh which range in taste from sweet to tart. The larger segment encases a seed which is bitter, so take care.

MANGO

Mangoes are favourites, with tastes ranging from tart to sweet. The thin, greenish-yellow-orange skin of the oval fruit surrounds yellowish-orange flesh and a large single seed. The mango should be cut lengthwise on both sides, with the knife kept as close as possible to the central seed. The flesh of the two cut pieces of mango should be cut in a criss-cross design without cutting the skin and the bottoms of the two pieces pressed upwards. Then the mango is ready for eating with a fork and/or spoon. Or it can just be picked up and enjoyed by biting into the juicy pulp. In an informal setting, the pulp surrounding the seed can also be enjoyed. One simply peels off the skin and picks up the seed to bite into the pulp. Eggshaped varieties of mango can be peeled. Make a small slit at the sharp end of the fruit and tear off strips of skin with the fingers. When the whole fruit is peeled, pick it up and bite into the succulent pulp.

LYCHEE

The brittle, red, outer covering of the small lychee, a native of South China, must be peeled off (using fingers is acceptable), before approaching the white, translucent, juicy flesh and one hard, oval seed.

LONGAN

The same applies to longans as to lychees. A longan is small and spherical, with a thin, brittle, light brown covering encasing white juicy pulp and a hard, round seed.

The pomelo, a native to South-east Asia, is the largest of the citrus fruits. The round fruit is covered with a rough, greenish-yellow skin and it has a thick pith. The skin should be cut in wedges barely touching the

POMELO

fruit of the pomelo and stopping short of the base. The thick skin is then peeled away revealing the fruit segments. The segments are covered with a papery skin which should be removed by making a slit on the skin and peeling it back to reveal the white or pink fruit sacs.

MANDARIN

A Mandarin is similar in appearance to an orange, but with the top and bottom slightly flattened. The skin is easily removed using thumbs and fingers. The membraneous, easily-separated, segments are orange in colour, sweet and juicy, and are eaten using the fingers. It is usual to remove any seeds from the mouth with the fingers and place the seeds on the discarded skin.

COCONUT

Coconut palms are plentiful in the tropics and coconut water is very refreshing. After drinking the liquid through a straw from the greenish-yellow fruit, the white fleshy meat can be scraped from the inside of the young coconut, using a long-handled spoon, and eaten. The coconut seller will prepare the coconut for the buyer, as it requires skill to cut the hard coconut open.

STARFRUIT

The golden starfruit or carombola, native to Java, is not only a thirst-quenching choice, but it is often seen in temples because of its shape and colour. It is best to remove the hard edge from each deep ridge before eating. When the fruit is sliced through, the star shape is revealed. Alternatively, the fruit may be cut in wedges along the troughs of the fruit. You may wish to remove the pith and seeds before eating.

Jambu air (water apple) is a small bell-shaped fruit ranging from white to green to bright pink. The fruit is often cut and dipped in dark soya sauce before eating.

The last two mentioned fruits are eaten with the skin intact, whereas the others must be peeled. Seeds are not edible in all cases (although the seeds of the durian and the jackfruit can be boiled and eaten).

In a restaurant, fruit is prepared in bite-size pieces, therefore forks and spoons or toothpicks will be available, for managing the cut fruit.

Hawker Centres

Hawker Centres provide informal settings for enjoying delicious Asian food with fast, unpretentious service at reasonable prices.

Many centres are situated outdoors, others are in markets and in easily accessible areas.

SEATING Tables and chairs are plentiful. You are at liberty to sit where you wish at the majority of hawker centres and order from several different stalls or hawkers. Sometimes, when tables and chairs are provided by an individual hawker, you are then expected to order from the hawker at whose table you are sitting. You mention your table number, or position, to the hawker from whom you are ordering, and the food will be served to your table.

SHARING A TABLE To share a table with strangers is acceptable, though one should first ask permission. In reply, an outstretched arm and hand pointing at the seat would indicate that the seat is available. Otherwise, say, "Sorry, the seat is taken."

Cash on delivery is usual. PAYMENT

The food is often shared amongst the party. That is, different dishes are ordered by those present and the food is distributed evenly to each person's individual plate, before commencing the meal. Or, the food from the central plates can be taken as and when wished throughout the meal by diners, bearing in mind the etiquette sensibilities of those eating. SHARING FOOD

Chopsticks may be used, or spoon and fork, or fingers, and crockery may be of disposable or plastic material. It is quite proper to use a spoon for the purpose of cutting food, if necessary. Rice is eaten from the spoon and the fork is used, concave side of the tines facing you, to push the food onto the spoon. UTENSILS

When sharing a table with strangers, the space occupied by your dishes should be kept to a minimum in order not to inconvenience others. SHARING TABLE SPACE

Empty plates and dishes, especially from different stalls, must not be stacked by diners upon finishing eating, as this may offend the religious, hygienic sensibilities of different stall holders. EMPTY PLATES

Expect to see the rules of etiquette relaxed in such centres, both in service and eating. Still the common acts of courtesy prevail, no matter how humble the setting.

Al fresco!

INDEX

NOTES